LOVE OF NATURE

~ *Natures Best* ~

GERI TUCHOLSKI

TRAFFORD
PUBLISHING™

Order this book online at www.trafford.com
or email orders@trafford.com

Most Trafford titles are also available at major online book retailers.

Printed in the United States of America.

ISBN: 978-1-4669-4562-3 (sc)
ISBN: 978-1-4669-4561-6 (e)

Trafford rev. 06/26/2012

 www.trafford.com

North America & international
toll-free: 1 888 232 4444 (USA & Canada)
phone: 250 383 6864 ♦ fax: 812 355 4082

Contents

Dedication

To my so Richard and my friend Vicky

I was inspire by my mother Edith Slay.

When I was 7 years old I love unity words down and they seem to sound alike then mom told me they rhyme, then I seen how exciting that seemed. So as my imagination grew I started rhyming words and lets neighbors read them. Its come so easy from there one. Now if finally came true. Thanks to my mother and son Richard who told me to go for it, and freed Victoria for paid for it. My dreams has come true I feel so part of the people who are author.

Thanks to everyone who had a part in the making of my book.
I love you all

Geri Tuchalsbi

To all my Family

I love my family
Thanks for all your love
I'll never forget you
And all the fun

My children are great
I love everyone
My grandchildren to
Finally met all, what love

I prayed for so long
Now I see
Its tare 2011
For you and me

Lets get together
For a party and fun
Then wall can see
Every son

Never worry

I never worry
About difference things
As far as I know
We can figure it out again

But things come around
To wonder about
But pleas don't worry
I'll see your around.

When things get better
The world will see
Now worrying is natural
For you and me.

But 2011, will be good
cause last year, was not
so pray everyday
and we'll get what we want.

The boat that sunk

A little boat sunk
In the sea
If I was with you
We could have freed

The boat from the water
The sails from the seas
Then you and I could go on and be.

How safety is good
Take bare of you boat
Then I'll never worry
About how it will float.

One Duckie

One little duckie
Sitting in a row
The little duckie
Said where do I go

There's no water
In the pond
So go inside
And get me some

Put little mo ousie
In the pond
Then you can come in
And have a lot of fun

My son

I mis you son
I miss gene to
You are the world to me
I love you both so true

Always remember
You're a great son
Your laughter, your smile
We always had fun

The day you left
I couldn't believe
How God could take you
And have you leave me.

You were bright and funny
A good guy around
I couldn't see how you didn't found
To stay at home I wish you did
Instead you wash your clothes
And it all had to end

Blue moon

The moon it sparkle
At night it looks right
I remember one day
We look at it at night

But the earth is perfect
The weather is grand
Why not come with me
Will have fun that was plans

The present

The present he gave me
The day we met
Was beautiful flowers
And a ring to match

They both sparkles
Cause sequin he got
And the ring and the flowers

Believe it or not
It's pretty to see
So always except flowers
A ring you can save

Winter

I hate the winter
To cold for me
I slip and slid
And fall down you see

The wind so cold
But pretty as can be
But winter to cold
And its not for me

So cozy inside
So we can see
Its either winter
Or inside with me

So I'll take the risk
Of going outside
Cause how else can I do this
Cause I surely can't hide

God

I love god and Jesus to
I pray every night
For me and you
God bless us just right

My savior is awesome
His free I adore
I couldn't love anyone
More and more

Your prayers are answered
Your life complete
Stay in his present
And you'll have a retreat

God loves you
And I do to
I'll be in your prayers
Till I see you adew

The water

The water the rain
It's pretty to see
If it wasn't for you
I wouldn't have rain

The sun can be nice
It's warm after the rain
See all that come
Can bring it again

I love spring the best of all
The summer pretty
Looks wise when it falls
So I like it all plenty

The river runs deep

The river is deep
With stones all in
Be careful when fishing
They'll hurt your feet, again again

The water looks pretty
It's blue with delight
If ever the river
Will go on and on tonight

Water and water runs so deep
Clear blue water
Easy to sleep
So always respect the deep

Water runs under a brook
Little fishes on a hook
Save the water live feel good
Come around any day. Will fish and goo

Listen

I listen to the birds
They sing so sweet
I like the colors
And they walk so neat

I listen to dogs bark
The kittens meow
Whose everyone to see
How listing a wow

The ocean, the wind
The children to booth
How can I listen
Without a flout to toot

I listen to children
There laughter so neat
I like the people
Who like to be sweet

The skies

The blue skies
The red rainbow
Are the prettiest colors
That I ever saw

I remember the stars
The clouds so blue
I remember always
Being with you

The silence are good
The breeze so sweet
If I ever was gone
I'd always remember you, a treat

The love hipe

I love life
As much as I can
I don't remember
Wherever we been

I has a grand life
Good children and friends
What ever happen
To good people, amen

We can't remember
But knows it true
I'll always be there
From me to you

The morrow

The marrow, your friend
The image you see
How nice you look
And how I can be

To dress to a tee
Be pretty and blue
Cause if you look new
He'll say, I love you

Your image with marrow
Reflex your life
But if you don't look
You really look nice

Every day

Every day
I wonder why
The birds always
Fly in the sky

There's pretty streams
The mountains so true
I wish the birds
Could fly by you

They make you happy
There pretty to booth
Play in the bird bath
And let us enjoy you

I love nature
The animal so dear
When there around
It's nice when there here

The river

The river is flowing
So deep and wide
Lets go fishing
You and i

We'll bate our hooks
A hear on the reel
While take the bug ones
Will call him Earl

The beginning of the week
The fish really bite.
My children love the river
Especially at night

One day

On a day I remember
I will be approved
One day
I love to be with you

I want a friend
Who's were and sweet
But what can you do
When no one thinks

Of things so dear
I only knew
Cause still one day
I'll be hear with you

The day I remember
Will come soon
The person I like
Is someone like you

The vision

For all to see
The life we lead
For all good things
Cause we were renube

We see vision
Though our eyes
So go fourth people
And look at the sky

So chose your eyes
For you to be
Why can't we all
Be free us a bee

The morning after
The reason is there
We don't do nothing
But see what's fair

All together

We get it all together
With everything we do
Especially when it goes around
And have someone like you

I rather be with you
For all the world to see
As I'm were as proud
As to be with you, by me.

I love you honey
No one compares
If I was a fruit
I'd be a pear

To be by you daily
To help you be fit
I'd eat a pear also
Cause first all the best

The Birds

The Birds in the sky
Are Beautiful to see
I watch them
And they watch me

The singing is pretty
It makes my day
Each day I wish
They come down to stay

The bluebird, the jaybird
The hawk and suck
There are so pretty
I believe there like ducks

For ducks and binds
Are all alike
Both like water
And eat seeds, to make them bright

Went to College

Went to college
For 2 yrs so far
Had problem with money
So now I have found

I have to quit
How said it is
For my other dream
To fit right in

I'm getting my poems done
So good to be there
It took 61 yrs
Now I have no fears

I always remember
My mom said to me
Always be parents
And things come to you
You'll see

My Kitten

I'm getting a kitten
I don't know when
But I really need one
For 2 was gone since then

The kitten are nice
So friendly you see
They give you friendly time
And always be with me

They purr, and scratch
On pole, and my shoes
But I really don't mind
Cause I love my cat so

There cuddly, so if, so sweet
There are so little
There feet are neat
There your friend, forever

My apt. has pretty pictures
High ceiling and more
I lived here 13 months
What more do I need to store

I'm ready to move
Wherever I don't know
Hope I find a place
Or I'll have no home

Please be careful
For there to do
Cause hard time are here
You might have lots of me
And no place to be near

Thankgiving

My thanksgiving day
Was pretty good
Friends came over
And cat my food

We laugh and chatted
For hours it seems
Then we talked thanksgiving
And all that it means

I prepared a nice meal
Punkin pie for desert
Then we all had a coke
To quench our thirst

The day was ended with a hug
Good buy be good
I hope you had fun
At your next one son

Writing Poems

I wrote so poems
To make a book
For people to enjoy
And a place to look

I enjoy the writing
I did it since age 7
So I hope you enjoy then
And will be all together

Enjoy all poems, and books
Once you did, you will see
It makes us smart
And then we can be

How sweet we become
And will be there
So open the poems book
And I'll be in a stare

My Mom

My mom was beautiful
A lady to me
She always was there
For everyone to see

She's honest and sweet
So understanding and kind
No one ever had
A nicer mom then mine

My children loved her
They did things you see
Once a month
Was for her and me

She died at age 83
Her heart was pure
She loved God
And she believe in the world

Our Restaurant

Our restaurant is nice
It brings our friends
So always remember
The happiness you been

The food is good
The people great
I'll always remember
We all have faith

So enjoy yourself
Eat hearty all day
Grow up healthy
And all behave

My grandchildren

I have 6 grandchildren
I love them all
I see 3 of them
The others I don't know

There ages are from 8-18
3 boys and 3 girls
I had 3 boys, and 1 girl
What a whirl

There all around me
I see only one
My daughter lives away
Can't see my other son

My Dog

I have a lab
She pretty as can be
If I lost her
How sad I would be

She's friendly and sweet
She loves everyone
So hope I don't ever
Forget who I got

I had 2 cats
For 5 yrs, or more
They got lost
And not found no more

3 yrs before that
I left ten behind
Found in the shelter
Turn out, there all mine

Pictures

My pictures of my son
Hanging on the wall
One when 18
The other when he was small

My son, he's 41
Has a picture with his son
I'll always hang them up
Till the wall falls

My children the greatest
I respect then to
Why can't they
Always, be with you

Playtime

My children when little
Always would play
The ball, the rope
Were there favorite all day

The swimming pool
Was a happy time
But what they like fine
Was a little prime

Always remember
The later we go
On happiness and laughter
And to go home

My play time is good
But what can we do
We all love playtime
And should be to

Ships

I like a ship with sails
The bay all shrug and new
But I like the best part
To be alone with you

I like a speed boat
To sale away
All comes together
And the waves will say

I like the water
The somberness I feel
The sun so bright
I will brake the seal

The Child

We love a child whose tidy
We love a child whose big
We love a child whose laughter
Sings in the heart of them

The play grounds in the back
Are fun time for all kids
I like to build a playgrounds
Who my friends to have them win.

We need the laughter
The fun to booth
But we all need something
To help us though

The Wind Blows

The sky has wind
It blows so sweet
It gets so windy
It blows me off my feet

The wind gives you comfort
To fill the air
I never retreat the day
It blows in my hair

To walk in the rain
Keep you cool and free
You can walk through the park
And have wind every day with me

The Earth

The earth so lovely the sky so blue you are the reason that I LOVE YOU.
The birds the bees, no one is better, for you and me, so we'll stick together
THE OCEANS NICE, THE WAVES SO HIGH, PLEASE SAY YOU'LL NEVER,
SAY GOODBYE.
I'm happy you love me, we roam through the day, everyone sees us, and say

all together

I'M ALTOGETHER, IN LOVE AND LIFE, I can spend a day, and also a night, with
my friends, my animals too, I HAVE TO CATS, I love them I DO.
SO REMEMBER THE REASON, I stay by your side, I WOULDN'T BE
ANYTHING, ALL THE DAYS THAT GO BY.

pretty flowers

THE FLOWERS THAT BLOOM, IN THE HEART OF THE DAY, WILL
ALWAYS LOOK PRETTY AND PEOPLE WILL SAY, LOOK AT THE
FLOWERS NOTHING CAN BEAT AND I GROW FLOWERS
SO PEOPLE CAN MEET. AROUND THE CORNER IN THE PARK
FLOWERS ARE PRETTY AND

roses

I LOVE ROSES THEY SMNELL SO SWEET YOU PICK THEM ALL IT
LOOKS SO NEAT PUT PERFUME ON THEM EACH FLOWER SMELLS OK
THEN IN THE WINTER THEY ALL GONE GO TO A MEADOW WHERE
FLOWERS ARE NICE ESPECIALLY ROSES WHERE THEY'RE NEVER OF
SITE.

The Garden

the flowers are pretty
in a garden so sweet
the flowers have senses
that are so neat.
the yellow, the red, the green and the blue
are filled with flowers, in a garden so true.
smell the garden
water the good
please remember I PLANTED THEM FOR YOU.

Breakthrough

the breakthrough for us
will be no more fear
no more war
to not be near
bring happiness to all
have laughter again
will all get together
go to heaven and then
no more heartaches
no more crying will be with GOD TILL THE END OF TIME

The skies

THE BLUE SKIES
THE RED RAINBOW
ARE THE PRETTIEST COLORS
THAT I ever saw
I REMEMBER THE SKIES
THE CLOUDS SO BLUE
I remember always being with you
the silence are good
the breeze so sweet
if I WAS EVER GONE
I'd always remember you as a treat.

Printed in the United States
By Bookmasters